MW00439720

I am sharing this with you because I care to share. @NCWiseman

Networking
for
Mutual Benefit

Teddy Burriss
aka
@NCWiseman

Copyright © 2013 Teddy Burriss

All rights reserved.

ISBN: 978-0-9889155-0-3

DEDICATION

Thanks to my beautiful & tolerant wife Rebecca, for pushing me to stay focused on completing this book.

CONTENTS

Acknowledgements

As with most people and their books, I also did not write this book on my own. Lots of people helped me make it happen.

I have met, and continue to meet, a lot of great people. Many have offered lots of encouragement and ideas for the things that I have done and accomplished in my life.

There is no way I can account for all of the people who encouraged me to write this book, the list is too freakin' long.

I know that my wife, Rebecca Burriss, has been my biggest encourager. I quit my job to start my business, and I dedicated Fridays to writing. She nearly beat me every time she saw something else show up on my calendar. "You will never get your books (oops spoiler) written if you don't get focused." Thanks, babe!

I met Nigel Alston in early 2010 and told him I wanted to write a book, despite not being a writer. He said two things, "You are a writer if you want to write," and "What is keeping you from finishing your book?"

Nigel and I met, talked or communicated through social media often. Each interaction started with one question, "Is your book done yet?"

He never told me to do it or lectured me for not having it done; he just asked that question. Thanks for "pushing," Nigel.

Nell Perry of the Forsyth Tech Community College Small Business Center was also a powerful contributor to this book becoming a reality. When I asked Nell to let me teach Networking for Mutual Benefit through the Small Business Center, she said yes. As of the spring of 2013, I have taught more than 250 individuals. Thanks for believing in me, Nell.

Chris Laney, Dena Harris and Kim Williams may not know it, but they also encouraged me to write through our conversations and their own examples.

They encouraged me to change the words I used when I talked about writing. I used to say "I'm not a writer, but I'm writing a book." I stopped saying this and started saying "I am a writer."

I also decided that I did not need to be perfect, but to just be. This helped me to keep going and complete the book.

Finally, I realized that by finishing this book I would be able to say "I am an author." And I can now proudly say this.

Introduction

I decided years ago that I should write this book for many reasons.

I believe so much in this message that I want everyone to hear it.

I travel the country sharing this message, and by having it documented in a book, I will be able to share it to far more people. It does not replace the public speaking and coaching work that I do. I love meeting new people and teaching them how to be more successful in life.

Another reason: I want to change the world. I used to think I couldn't do this.

Now I believe I can.

Maybe only one person at a time, but I truly believe that if I share the message to enough people it will help them to accept and live this new lifestyle of networking. A friend of mine told me that by teaching good stuff to good people I will create a team of evangelists, and they will share the message as well, thus helping change the world. I see this happening already.

The most important reason for writing this book is that I want you to know that there is a better way to succeed.

I measure success by the relationships I build in life. I have learned that I can build relationships that help me to be successful in my business and life. This lifestyle has opened doors for me and allowed me to help others who, in turn, have helped me. It's a never-ending circle of success that only occurs when I stay TRUHE (transparent, relevant, useful, honest and engaging) and trust in a lifestyle I call "Networking for Mutual Benefit." When I deviated from this lifestyle, I saw my business success falter. As soon as I got back on track with real Networking for Mutual Benefit, the benefits returned, and life was much better. (see my successes)

I like being different, especially when different is better. Differentiation is important in a world filled with commodities. I don't want to be a commodity, nor do I want to be put on a list with other "typical" people. Being typical or a commodity does not lead to benefits. Networking is what everyone else does. I don't; I Network for Mutual Benefit.

Please, read this book and join me in being different and better.

Discovering Networking

My First Sales Job

In 2005 I began feeling that the job I was doing no longer suited me. I loved the company and the people I worked with. They paid me well, gave me lots of freedom to work in the community and time to spend with my family. These are all important issues to me, but I was no longer excited about the work itself.

While looking for a new career idea, I discovered a sales job that seemed interesting. I talked with the owner of the business numerous times and eventually took his job offer. It's important to know that I did not have a resume, did not fill out an application and did not get a background check or drug test. I got this job based on what the owner knew about me. More on this later.

This was my first sales job. I knew that there had to be at least one activity that would make or break my new sales career. So on my first day on the job, I asked my new boss to tell me the one activity that if I did well I would be successful for his business.

He said, "Grip and grin your way through every networking event, collect tons of business cards, call all of them relentlessly and ask them to buy our stuff."

This disturbed me. I was not excited about this "grip and grin" thing. I also doubted that cold calling a big list of phone numbers would create any real or lasting success for me or the business. It's not that I knew this based on real-life experience. I based my opinion on my own reaction to sales folks cold-calling me. I hated getting those calls, and I was not eager to subject others to stuff I hated. I live the Golden Rule, "Do unto others what you would have them do unto you," and forcing cold calls on others contradicted this rule.

Of course I had to do what my boss wanted. I needed that paycheck he promised me each month, and, in order for me to get it, I needed him to feel as if I were successful. So I did what he said.

I joined networking groups across the Triad area of North Carolina. I attended breakfast before hours and breakfast after-hours events. I became a networking wild man. I began attending all of the local Chamber of Commerce events, business expos and seminars. I broke a company record by handing out nearly 1,000 business cards in less than six months. My boss was excited at all of my activity.

I collected so many business cards that it took me hours every Friday to enter them all into our (C)ustomer (R)elationship (M)anagement system.

I crafted a powerful and informative 30-second commercial that I rehearsed so many times that I often dreamt it.

I scheduled one-on-ones with dozens of sales folks who sold to the same businesses I wanted to sell to.

I crafted fantastic cold-calling and voicemail scripts that I used all day long.

I lived by my calendar, which was filled with networking, one-on-one meetings, cold-calling schedules and time to manage my lists of business cards.

In the next few chapters, I'll talk about what I

discovered about networking, cold calling and one-on-one meetings.

Networking is a dirty word

Yes, lots of people like to network to collect business cards and to find that one person they can talk with about their products, services and business.

However, there are far more people who think networking is a dirty word.

There are many different perspectives of networking.

Some people don't like to do it because of the negative perception that they have about networking. They believe it's an activity for sales people only.

Some people are afraid of meeting new people, so they don't like networking either. They're either afraid of asking a stranger questions or that the stranger will ask a question that they can't answer.

Another group of people don't want to be added to cold-calling lists, email marketing lists and become a big target for sales people, so they won't network and share their contact info with anyone. Usually, these are the company executives who only want to run their businesses. They expects their staffs to do the networking work.

Many people don't want to trapped in a conversation with an overwhelming, pushy person. It can be stressful finding an "out" when this happens. I have seen people shudder in fear when faced with this.

Because of these fears, networking is considered a

dirty word to many, including me. Because of that, many who start networking will either quit completely or make up excuses not to participate. It's an activity that our young business leaders, future entrepreneurs and students want to leave alone. And I don't blame them. Based on what I went through, I don't want to be a part of that again.

Even today I am assaulted by this style of networking, although I can now deal with all of the fears of typical networking.

Our bosses tell us that networking helps us find people who will buy our stuff. My boss was so happy that I came back from networking events and individual prospecting meetings with tons of business cards and new targets to "sell" our stuff to.

The activities that I think give networking a bad rap include the "30-second commercial," "you're talking but I'm not listening," "business-card swap meets" and "giving referrals and leads to and from strangers."

Brought to you by commercials

We have been told repeatedly that 30-second (even 60-second and longer) commercials are our defining statements. We are taught that it's important to first tell people what job we have, and that we must start every conversation with these commercials.

Because we have been trained this way, every networking event is a giant hum of these commercials. Dozens, if not hundreds, of people are doing the same thing, gripping and grinning as many people as we can and spewing our 30-second commercial out. Eventually, a listener will need what we have to sell.

Commercials like:

"Hi, I'm Steve Salesman. I work for Company XYZ, and I sell wireless thing-a-ma-jigs. We have been in business for 80 years and are the industry leader in providing the shiniest and quietest thing-a-ma-jigs in the world. Our thing-a-ma-jigs are made in the USA and come with lifetime warranties. A good lead for me is anyone you know who needs thing-a-ma-jigs or uses old-style battery-operated do-wokers."

Often these 30-second or 60-second commercials drone on so much longer, and we let our minds drift away. We think about whatever pops into our heads or our eyes catch sight of something in the room that we begin thinking about instead of what is being said. We look at our smartphones in hopes of an important email or text to escape to. If we make any movement or indication that we want to know more about thing-a-ma-jigs (which, of course, we don't), we get even more noise about the stuff Steve Salesman sells.

I refer to this rambling about your products and services, features, benefits and noise about your company as "barfing."

As our interest in the thing-a-ma-jigs diminishes and before Steve Salesman finishes barfing, we can see him scanning the room for others he wants to assault with his commercial in hopes that someone out there may be interested in his wireless thing-a-ma-jigs.

Once Steve Salesman feels comfortable he has barfed enough (for now) about his business, he'll likely ask to do the business-card swap. More about this later.

There are some Steve Salesmen out there who are so into themselves and their wiz-bang business that they never give you the opportunity to spew your commercial back on them. We called these folks networking jerks. We all know who they are, and we stay clear of them.

If Steve does ask who you work for, it's likely because his hors d'oeuvres are getting cold or he needs to catch his breath. Or because he has already barfed all over you and found no apparent interest, his interest in anything you have to say is so minuscule, he has already checked out of the conversation. He has a laser beam on his next suspect and is waiting for an opportunity to move on.

You're talking but I'm not listening

We were taught to barf our commercials on as many people as possible, even if they aren't listening.

As we begin to reciprocate and throw up our 30-second commercial all over Steve Salesman, we can tell he's not listening. Every now and then, he looks in our direction, but only for a millisecond or two, as he scans the room for his next victim. Steve Salesman will utter a polite "Really?" or "Interesting" response, but he clearly isn't listening to anything we are saying. Because he's already barfed all over us, he is focused on one thing, and one thing only — getting away from us in order to get to that next victim, er, person.

While we drone on and on about our products and services or sometimes even the features and benefits of our products, Steve Salesman is searching for someone he believes needs his stuff. This would be the Holy Grail of tonight's networking. Steve Salesman's boss would be ecstatic if he hears that Steve barfed his 30-plus-second commercial on this guy. Finding this person will make Steve's night. It would be the prize he needs to compensate him for the time he spent barfing all over us.

Once he finds this guy in the room, the dance changes drastically. Steve Salesman's face lights up, and he becomes more engaged in our discussion. However, the increased engagement is clearly intended to get to the end of our time together. As the target moves around the room, Steve will also move around us so that he can keep an eye on his supposed prize. We have to shuffle too so that we can continue to face Steve Salesman as we spew our stuff all over him.

Even though it's clear that Steve Salesman has completely tuned out our commercial, we never ask him, "Are you listening to me?" We know the moment we say those words, the room will come to a complete stop and everyone will look at us. We are smarter than that. Networking was not about being listened to; it's only about barfing out our commercials on as many people as possible.

The Business Card Swap Meet

To many, networking events are nothing more than business-card swap meets.

Our bosses love to buy business cards. They want these 2" x 3.5" billboards to be considered keepsakes by the people we give them to. Our bosses believe that every business card we gave out is still lying on top of the desk of the people we gave them to.

They want us to hand them out everywhere we go, and if we can give someone two or three cards, that's even better. We believe that giving out business cards increases the number of people who will know how to contact us once they realize they need to buy our stuff. And since our cards are right there in front of everyone, the phone will start ringing real soon.

Our bosses wanted us to collect business cards, too. The more business cards we brought back to the office, the happier they were. There was nothing better than a slap on the back and a "good job" statement from the boss when he saw the pile of cards we collected. We were happier than pigs in slop sitting in front of our cold-calling system and entering all of the cards we collected from the week's networking. After we entered them into the system we would do a virtual high-five with ourselves, proud of all the work we had done. When we got done entering them all in, we would put the paper business cards in our business-card portfolio, sort of like our trophy box for business cards.

Going to a networking event without your business

cards is a major failure. People will talk about you, "He's here, and he has no business cards with him. What a shame." You almost want to crawl into a corner and not network at all when this happens.

While networking, swapping business cards can be considered an indication that you want to get back together to reconvene barfing all over each other. Just as frequently it could mark the end of the barfing so that you can each get back to trolling for that next suspect or hunt down that Holy Grail we saw earlier.

At every networking event, it is fully assumed when you hand another person your business card that they are going to cold call you relentlessly and add you to their email and newsletter campaigns, despite your needs or relevance to their stuff. You accepted this and hoped whoever gave you their business card would accept as well.

There is another group of networking folks who pass out and collect business cards. These folks don't know about follow-up. They will take their bounty of business cards home and never do anything with them. To all of us who show up at networking events, this is a slap in the face.

The business-card swap is a measure of success. Bring back a bunch of business cards that you can enter into your cold-calling machine, and you are successful. Hand out so many cards that you have to order more, and you are successful. You could be awarded the coveted salesman-of-the-week award if you gave out the most business cards and collected the most business cards all in the same week.

Passing Referrals and Leads to and From Strangers

Regardless of what you know of the people in your networking group or about the business they represent, be ready to provide referrals and leads.

Join a networking group that meets weekly, and you will be strongly encouraged (or required) to participate in the time-honored sharing of referrals and leads. These groups have what they refer to as single product/service seats. This means that anyone providing the same product or service that other members of the group provide will not be allowed to join the group.

Regardless of how well you know (not to mention trust or respect) your networking group members, let alone what you know about (again, trust or respect) their company, everyone is expected to fill out the referral and leads forms and to pass them back and forth between each other.

Referrals are the full-contact information of businesses/individuals that you suspected to currently need the products/services that one of your networking group members provided. Leads were supposed to be businesses/individuals that used similar services/ products that one of your networking group members provided, even if they were already using these products/services from other sources.

Most networking groups suggest that the members

schedule one-on-one meetings to get to know "What are good leads for you?" They encouraged the members to get to know each other in order to have a clear understanding of their business and networking goals. Yet the passing of referrals and leads must occur regardless.

I hate this requirement. I want to share leads and referrals with people I trust and respect, people I have some level of a positive relationship with.

Networking sucks

I have done typical networking. I've been involved in networking groups, and I've passed referrals and leads back and forth with people I did not know well. Because I have done all of this, I can honestly testify that networking sucks!!

I truly believe that the "30-second commercial," "you're talking but I'm not listening," "the business-card swap meets" and "passing referrals and leads to and from strangers" are the activities that have turned networking into a dirty word.

I have repented and begged for forgiveness from those I networked with. Many have forgiven me because they know that I have repented and shown that I am better than this.

But these are not my worst social sins. Networking led to other activities that leave me embarrassed and apologetic.

Business Card Ritual

A well-executed networking event can yield you dozens of business cards for your cold-calling system. I scheduled Friday afternoons to enter these cards into our system. I did this for two reasons: This work made for an easy Friday afternoon, and if I needed, I could do it from my home office or from my laptop at a bar with Wi-Fi. (Did I just admit to that? Oops.)

Either way, collecting the business cards and getting them entered into our system was just the start of lots of work that I hated even more.

The Cold-Calling Ritual

The definition of "cold calling" is to "make a telephone call to someone who does not expect your call, does not know anything about you, does not know what your business is and has no specific or current need for your products or services."

Look at the breakdown of this definition:

Does not expect your call;

Does not really know you (OK, you met at a networking event, but remember, no one really listens);

Does not know what your business/products/ services are;

Has no specific or current need for your products or services;

Is perturbed at the interruption.

Why would anyone want to make this call? Why would anyone want to take this call?

Truth be told, neither the caller or the called wants to participate in this ritual.

Our bosses know that we hate to cold call. They try to make it a game, a challenge or a major event of the week with the hopes that we will enjoy it at least enough to get through the task. They give out prizes for the most cold calls in the first hour, a gift card for the first one with an appointment and more prizes for other goals met each hour of the blitz. Sometimes these prizes worked wonders. Often, they were not enough to excite the entire team to cold call better, faster and more successfully.

Besides the breakdown of the definition of cold calling, there are some really big reasons why most sales people despise cold calling:

The Script - Often the sales manager or marketing staff would write the cold-call script we used, especially during blitz calls. It was intended to get the point of the call out so that the person we called was clear on the purpose of our call as quickly as possible. A well-crafted script had branches of discussion points based on the responses we got. However, few companies understood how to do branching. This left it up to us to figure out how to deal with the varied responses we got. Most of us hated cold-call scripts.

Don't accept "No!" - Our boss told us to do everything we could to get a meeting with the people we called. There was a five-dollar McDonald's gift card for each appointment we set. This was far more difficult than he thought. The people we were calling, again for the most part because of the above definition, did not want to meet with us. They had no need for our products/services; they were busy with other issues, and we were interrupting them. They already had someone doing the same thing for them already, or any of a dozen other reasons not to meet with us. Yet we were unyielding and not going to accept a "no."

We were conditioned to take on every objection with either the branched discussion points or our own freewheeling responses. I remember jumping from one product set to another with each objection I received. Like a well-oiled machine, I doled out option after option, product set after product set to each and every "no" I heard until I got tired or the person on the phone stopped responding or got so angry that they were on the verge of hanging up the phone. Often after pressing harder than I should have, I either got an angry "NO!", a hang up or, worse yet, a "take me off your calling list."

At least nine times out of 10, we had to accept either "no" or a "no" with expletives wrapped around it. Most humans, even sales people, hate to hear the word "no."

Leaving a Message - Good (loose use of this word) cold-calling scripts were crafted with a real life person script and an answering machine (later renamed to voicemail or VM) script. The VM script was an encouragement for the owner of the voice mailbox to call us back. It usually did not reference our company name or products/services. The only intent of a VM script was for them to call us back. Unfortunately, one of two things generally happened with VM scripts. They would not call back, or they would call back and discover that it was a sales call, and they would quickly get to "no." Either way, leaving a message nearly never resulted in a positive next step. This always seemed like a total waste of time.

The Gatekeeper - It's a challenge getting past the gate keeper.

This is often a lady trained to keep all sales people at bay. If there was a gatekeeper involved, you could never get to the voicemail, let alone to the person you were calling. Gatekeepers could care less about your products or services. They cared even less about features and benefits or how long your company has been in business. They care about one thing - keeping you away from their boss. Sometimes the schmoozing worked, but a good gatekeeper was unwavering at her job.

I remember some sales coaching related to gatekeepers. Stuff like sweet talking the gatekeeper, convincing the gatekeeper that their boss wanted her to let us get in touch with them, that we were following up from morning coffee or lunch (maybe not completely true) or that we were different than most sales people and only wanted to help her boss.

Call Cycle - Stay top of mind, and they'll eventually buy. If the first time they said no, if they did not return our call, if the gatekeeper said "no", then we had to keep trying. Our cold-calling system had a feature to schedule the next call. Everyone had a different idea of Call Cycle. Weekly, monthly, quarterly? It always seemed that the more quotes we were sending out the longer the call cycle to everyone else. If we were desperate to fill the pipeline, we'd increase the cycle to weekly. All this seemed to do for us was to increase the opportunities for no, voicemail and gatekeeper activities. Rarely did it increase the quoting or proposal activity. In summary, it just made us all unhappy because our cold-calling activity was not growing our business.

Use other paths - When we had the email addresses and mailing addresses of our targets, we would adjust our cold-calling activity. Everyone thought it was great to be able to assault our targets by phone, email and snail mail. Adding their email addresses to our weekly marketing campaigns for email and brochure mailings was just another way to keep us top of mind with them. Often, all it did was make our targets more aggressive with the "no" because they were getting fed up with the multi-front assault.

I don't want to state sales facts and figures about appointment setting rates or actually business done on this activity. For me, it was pretty slim. I am sure that my appointment setting rates were less than ten percent of each cold call, spam email or letter. The actual business done through this activity was a fraction of the appointments I actually got through this activity.

The cold-calling ritual has been around forever as a key step in the sales process. I doubt that people will stop doing it. At least not until they learn a new idea.

One-on-One Dance

Often, networking in groups leads to what are called "one-on-one" meetings with the people we meet. Usually, these meetings were with other sales people, not necessarily potential clients.

We usually scheduled these meetings around coffee or lunch, sometimes after work. We'd talk about ourselves a little, the weather, politics and/or sports. After a little chitchat, we'd get down to business.

This is what was considered the core of a good one-on-one meeting.

We would talk about the last networking event and our success collecting business cards there. We'd talk about who we saw, who we did not see and who was there that we could not get to. We would compare notes for upcoming networking events and arrange to see each other at the next event.

Sometimes, we would practice our 30- or 60-second commercials on each other and accept "constructive" comments hoping to fine-tune this commercial. It was always useful to have someone with a really good 30-second commercial to listen to ours and give us ideas of how to improve barfing activity.

We would take turns showing each other our shiny brochures and slick demo slides that we carried around in the backseats or trunks of our cars. Sometimes we would look at each other's web sites and online ads. Often we would trade our promotional materials, pens, cups, mouse pads, etc. If our new networking buddy had cooler stuff, we would take whatever he gave us back to the office. We would marvel at the great graphics and really cool presentations of each other's stuff and wish for the day we could have really neat marketing material.

It was also expected that you bring your "contact list" to these meetings. We would go down through the list looking for names of companies and individuals on each other's list. We'd get excited when we would see a name of a business or individual that we considered a great target for ourselves. We'd highlight each other's list and ask "Will you introduce me to him, please?" Almost without fail, we all agreed to introduce each other to anyone we had contact information for.

We would trade out business cards again, sometimes giving out multiple cards with the intent of looking for someone else to give our friend's card to. We thought this was a great way to help our new friends get more connections.

We usually bought our own coffee, sweet tea or after-hours "soda" during these one-on-one meetings. However, if you thought you would get some really good connections out of this meeting, you would pick up the entire tab. Heck, you could expense it anyway.

After these one-on-one meetings, we would go back to our offices and fire off emails to our connections, regardless of our relationship with them. Messages like this:

"Hello, Customer Charlie. My good buddy Steve Salesman works for Company XYZ, and they sell wireless thing-a-ma-jigs. They have been in business for 80 years and are the industry leader in providing the shiniest and quietest thing-a-ma-jigs in the world. Their thing-a-ma-jigs are made in the USA and come with lifetime warranties. I think you and Steve the Salesman should meet. Can I help arrange coffee or lunch with the three of us?"

Sound familiar? It's Steve Salesman's 30-second commercial rebroadcast by one of his networking buddies. One of the big goals of the one-on-one ritual was to be able to do this. This was considered a success.

I was not interested in meetings like this or having my new connections introduce me to their contacts in such an ugly way.

I know there is a much more enjoyable and beneficial one-on-one process.

Stop the insanity

In the spring of 2006, about one year into my sales career, I was doing OK selling IT solutions. I was making OK money, and I enjoyed the freedom I had and the people I was connecting with. But I was not happy.

It all seemed so phony. I kept looking at what I was doing and eventually came to this realization. There were three things that I hated doing:

#1 Not For Me Activity - I no longer wanted to be "gripping and grinning my way through networking events collecting business cards." Everyone knew that handing out your business card in a networking event meant you would be put on a cold-calling or email-blasting list. I didn't want people treating me this way, and I surely didn't want to considered "one of those guys" by people I did this to. I really did not want to degrade my personal brand with the people in my network by being this kind of a networker.

#2 Not For Me Activity - I no longer wanted to cold call with the hopes of becoming successful. I did not fear cold calling, voicemail black holes, gate keepers or the word "no." I have always had pretty tough skin and broad shoulders. What I did not like was the waste of my valuable time doing something that I considered to be of minimal value. I knew that I could use that time for much more beneficial activities.

#3 Not For Me Activity - I did not want to become a leech and use one-on-one meetings to grope my way through other people's contact lists. I feel violated when some of the people I meet during one-on-ones, often for the first time, want me to introduce them to everyone I know with no regard of relationship or relevance.

My desire to grow my pipeline and sales did not mean I had to do this stuff that I despised. My reputation is important to me, and I did not want to tarnish it by being considered a typical "salesman." I wanted to be unique. I wanted people to see me coming into a room or even down the street and for them to want to say hello to me.

I needed to come up with a new way to do my job; otherwise, I was going to quit and do something other than sales.

So I picked up my pace finding a new way to do my job.

I thought you were a salesman

I got serious about modifying my networking activity after a lunch appointment with a distant business friend.

I had not seen Bill in quite some time and thought it would be fun to have lunch with him. I knew he was recently unemployed and knowing what he did for a living, maybe I could help him find a job.

Early one morning, I called Bill and invited him to lunch, my treat. For reasons initially unknown to me, he was reluctant to say yes. I finally convinced him to do lunch, but I could tell he was worried about something.

We met at a sub shop not far from where Bill lives. We exchanged quick and simple "hellos" in line while we ordered our subs. Once we sat down at the table, I let him talk about losing his job. I asked simple questions about his family. After he reminded me he was married with one daughter, we talked about his wife and daughter. He was really proud of his daughter and the work his wife does. We talked more about losing his job and lots more about stuff that he likes, such as wood carving, his community, a little politics, art and kayaking.

Bill asked me about my business, and I told him that business was good and that I was enjoying the work and the people I get to meet and work with. I politely and quickly stopped talking about myself and asked him what he was planning for his job search. We talked about this for awhile, and he even brought up his fear of losing his home and/or savings. We talked about what he wanted to do, and I quickly learned enough to be able to introduce him to some people who I thought may be able to help him find a job.

He asked me a few more questions about my job, and I told him a little more about my business and what I was doing to help others. I did not tell him about the specific products and services my business provides; he was not interested in that.

We talked about going kayaking on Salem Lake in Winston-Salem, N.C., and about some of the other people we mutually knew, some really good friends, others good business contacts. We both know a lot of people, and a traditional networker would have been taking down names and asking for introductions. I didn't even consider this.

As we ended our time together, I promised to introduce him to some good people who could possibly help him. I made sure that Bill knew that these people did not have job openings, but they know lots of other in the same industry and would be able to introduce him to others who may know about job openings.

He thanked me for the lunch and my offer to help him. He then asked, "What can I do to help you?"

I said, "If you know anyone who may have an interest in what my business does or may know someone who can help me make more good business connections, please introduce me to them."

"I'll do that," he said. "You have helped me more than you know, and all you did was listen to me."

Before we got up I asked, "Why were you so reluctant

to come to lunch with me?"

Here is the quote that smacked me right in the middle of my eyes: "I was afraid, that because you are a salesman, you'd want to sell me something."

He added, "But now I realize you didn't want to sell me anything. You wanted to get to know me better so that you can help me. Thanks."

I thanked him for the kind words and said, "Look, Bill, I want to help you because you are a good guy. And besides, who knows, one day in the future, you'll be able to help me. But that's not important to me right now. I just want to help a friend."

Wow - I heard what he said, and I understood what it meant.

He thought I was calling on him to sell him something. I was embarrassed; I had never thought about trying to sell him anything and wondered how he came up with that idea. Had my reputation been diminished to being a "salesman?"

Note: I mean no disrespect towards sales professionals, retail sales folks and others responsible for selling products and services to the public. I use the phrase "salesman" as in the great movies and literary pieces that depict the seersucker suits, slicked-back hair and a cadre of one-liners focused on going for the kill, I mean, sale.

I was really happy that I was able to help him, initially just by listening, but equally as important with the introductions I made for Bill that eventually led him to starting his own business.

It was the last phrase he said that hit home. "You wanted to get to know me better so that you can help." That was powerful to me.

As I thought about this statement, I reminded myself that I was now being who I wanted to be, not who others thought I should be.

I truly wanted to learn more about Bill and find a way to help him.

I had no desire to get his contact information and cold-call him.

I did not have the urge to barf my 30-second commercial on him to find business.

I never thought about scrounging through his contacts to find someone for him to introduce me to.

This reminded me of a quote I wrote years ago. "It's not that I was being different than I wanted to be, I was just being different than what others wanted me to be."

The memory of this lunch meeting has stuck with me for years, and it helped move me further down the road of making more changes in my life.

Discovering new Ideas

Toastmasters

In the late 1990s, my job required that I speak to groups of people about the projects that I was working on. It required that I answer spontaneous questions about many topics, some totally irrelevant to the initial conversation or presentation. And it required me to have good leadership skills for the team that worked with me.

I was able to do this work when I started the job, but once I joined Toastmasters I began to bet much better at all of these tasks. My improved speaking and leadership skills were quite apparent to everyone I worked with. Furthermore, I began enjoying my job more as well.

While putting together a plan for a new style of networking, I recounted my involvement in Toastmasters and a conversation I had with a good friend.

In 2001 I joined a Toastmasters Club in Winston-Salem. Toastmasters is a great place to improve your public speaking, impromptu speaking skills and leadership skills. I loved Toastmasters and stayed in this group for five years.

There were two couples, good friends, in this club who were focused on the same task. They wanted to help the new members of their club become great toastmasters. All four were clearly dedicated to this work.

These four people helped to train and coach me to become a good toastmaster as well. I'd say I became a great toastmaster, but I still deal with uhms and ahs and the clock.

They gave me speech ideas and evaluated my speeches and table topics by paying attention to what I said and how I said it. Their constructive feedback helped propel me along my journey of becoming a competent toastmaster. I had a fabulous time and learned lots from these good folks. This experience changed my life.

To this day, I thank these people for the significant improvement in my job and life that they and my involvement in Toastmasters created. These good people helped me immensely, and they also became friends.

What was the most amazing is that they did all of this with no expectations of anything in return.

Looking back at the four years I spent in Toastmasters, I don't recall either of them asking me for anything outside of the club activities. Nothing. They only wanted to help whomever and wherever they could. And because they helped all of us in the club so much, none of us ever turned them down when asked to pitch in on any task related to the club. I held numerous leadership roles in this club because they asked me to do so.

This intrigued me. These two couples were successful in their careers and lived good lives. They had an untold numbers of friends and loved what they did in their jobs and communities. They gave their time and experience to anyone who needed help, again with no expectations of anything in return.

One day I arrived early to a Toastmasters meeting. I sat and had a bowl of soup with one of these good folks. We chatted for a few minutes before I found a way to ask her, very politely, "Why do you do so much for this club and not expect anything in return?"

"I get rewarded every day for the work I do in this club," she said. "Every day, someone does something nice or important for me. It may not be a club member, and sometimes it's someone I have not talked to in weeks or months. I know that when I show up and give to my club, I will get rewarded. I never expect it; I just know it happens."

I am sure that the other three club members who gave to the club every day felt the same way. I did not need to ask.

Her reply added more insight into an idea I was working on.

Successful Business Leaders share ideas

An idea was coming together for a new style of networking. I needed to find out what other successful people were doing that I may not be doing, or what I was doing and could do better at.

In Winston-Salem, I knew some successful business leaders. These were people who I trusted and respected, not for how much money they made, the type of car they drove or suits they wore, but rather because they are involved in their communities, were eager to help others and because other folks I knew trusted and respected these people as well. I called a few of these business leaders and asked if we could do coffee or lunch so that I could ask them an important question about themselves. As I expected, they all said "Yes." I scheduled coffee with one and lunch on the same day with another.

My first meeting was with a guy I will call Jim. We met at a small coffee shop in downtown Winston-Salem. I had a great time with Jim. We talked about all kinds of interesting stuff, our families, communities, friends, the local economy and some of the volunteer work we each did. We discovered that we were connected to some other interesting and successful people.

We talked about lots of other interesting topics, like the kinds of coffee we each liked best, articles we had read online and some of the books we had read and thought the other would enjoy.

During our chat, I asked Jim, intending to be funny, "What do you do to entertain yourself Monday through Friday?" In very simple words Jim said, "I'm the VP of marketing for Company XYZ. It's very rewarding work, especially since our company is a fun place to work."

Then Jim asked me, "What kind of work do you do?" I did not barf out my typical 30-second commercial. Instead I said, "I'm an IT consultant. It's fun work, especially when I can help a business owner find new ideas that help his business grow."

We talked a little about how we got into our respective careers. It was an interesting conversation. Both of us got our jobs because of the people we knew, not our resumes or interviewing skills.

Then I said, "I wanted to get together with you because I respect you in regards to both your community involvement and your business. From my perspective, I consider you successful in both areas. Will you share with me the most important thing you did to achieve your success?"

Jim did not hesitate. "Thank you for noticing, Teddy. Without a doubt, the most important thing to me is the people in my life. Besides hard work and a good team, everything else is a byproduct of these relationships."

This made sense to me.

We chatted some more about what success is and is not.

At the end of our time together, we agreed to stay in touch, and if either of us needed anything, we agreed to get back together.

Later, my lunch meeting was with a nice guy named John. I've known John for a long time, and we see each other in the community at various charitable and public events. Oddly, we had never sat down and talked.

John has a successful consulting business and seems so busy that I was surprised he had time for lunch.

We met at a noisy sandwich shop. Both of us had been there numerous times, so there was no need to spend time delving into the menus. We ordered our favorite lunches and sat down.

Our conversation wasn't much different than my chat with Jim earlier.

We talked about family, friends, our communities and maybe a little more about sports than Jim and I did. Turns out that John was a football player in college. As with Jim, John and I discovered that we were involved in similar activities and had lots of the same connections.

John asked me to tell him what I did for a living, and I asked him the same question I put to Jim, "What do you do to entertain yourself Monday through Friday?" John laughed and said he never thought of it that way, but everything he did for a living was actually entertaining to him; otherwise he would have quit it years ago.

We joked a little about some of the new TV sitcoms that neither of us spent much time watching, yet we did have our own favorites. Neither of us watched any TV news or reality TV shows. Both of us liked good comedies that made us laugh long and hard.

Finally, I asked John the same question that I had put to Jim, "What do you consider to be the most important thing that helped you become successful in your life and career, John?"

Like Jim, John did not pause. "It's the relationships I develop with people, Teddy. Not just knowing them, but really getting to know who they are and what's important to them. My life would have been different if I had not worked hard at building relationships with people. Nothing else compares to the importance of building relationships. Yeah, I have to work hard and make good choices, but the relationships I have created in life are the most important reason for my success."

We talked a little longer about meeting people and how to get to know someone well enough to know how to help him before our time ran out.

Again, not unlike my meeting with Jim, John offered this statement, "If there is anything else I can do to help you, Teddy, please just give me a call."

I politely and honestly offered the same back to John.

I later had the pleasure of sharing meals with two successful business leaders in my town, and they had similar ideas. They didn't harp on their jobs or ask me for anything. They both offered to help me any way they could. We shared ideas and conversations about all kinds of topics and got to know each other better.

This made sense to me. We were building relationships.

And my ideas were starting to really come together.

Sandler Sales Training

While I worked on my plan, I kept thinking about a training program I had gone through in 2003.

Sandler Sales Training President's Club was an eighteen-week course that met every few weeks. There were nearly fifty people in the class. The trainer, a guy named Bob, was an in-your face, loud and excited guy. He kept telling us to learn the principles, not his style. This was important because most of the attendees could never see themselves doing what Bob did.

I learned a lot about sales during my Sandler Training classes. Much of what I learned was focused on the sales process. It's important to remember that the sales steps are important, when the time is right. Selling is not a part of the Networking for Mutual Benefit activities, as you will learn later in this book.

One of the segments of the Sandler training was called Bonding & Rapport. The training in this section really made sense to me, even though I thought it was a not quite focused on building a real, long-lasting relationship. I learned that you must create some level of a bond and have a mutually trusting and respectful rapport with anyone you are trying to sell to.

As I studied this section of the training, I learned the value of the word "mutual" as a business word, as in mutual trust, mutual respect, mutual concern and mutual understanding. I collapsed these words into "mutually beneficial." In order to have mutual trust, respect, concern and understanding, the relationship must allow for mutual benefit.

I enjoyed and learned a lot from the Sandler Training. I still have the CDs, and I listen to them now and then, especially the Bonding & Rapport section.

During my journey to find a better way to become successful, the concepts of Sandler's Bonding & Rapport seemed to fit well into the idea I was developing.

It was all coming together well. I knew there was a better way to network and sell successfully.

Dale Carnegie Training

Years ago, likely while I was still in school, one of my professors told me about a guy named Dale Carnegie. I did not pay much attention back then, but the name Dale Carnegie kept coming up as I worked to be successful. So I thought I better find out who this guy is.

I "Googled" Dale Carnegie and found the books that some of my friends had mentioned to me. The number-one selling book by Dale Carnegie was "How to Win Friends and Influence People." I had a Kindle back then, so I bought the digital book and started reading it.

It took me a month to get through the book. But, wow, I learned a lot.

Dale Carnegie had two famous maxims (or rules of conduct).
The first was to "Believe that you will succeed and you will."
The second one was, "Learn to love, respect and enjoy other people."

These maxims made a lot of sense to me and seemed easy to do.

Dale Carnegie also collapsed much of what he wrote in his book "How to Win Friends and Influence People" in a small booklet called "Dale Carnegie's Golden Book."

There are nine principles in a section titled "Become a Friendlier Person."

They are:

1. Don't criticize, condemn or complain.
2. Give honest, sincere appreciation.
3. Arouse in the other person an eager want.
4. Become genuinely interested in other people.
5. Smile.
6. Remember that a person's name is to that person the sweetest and most important sound in any language.
7. Be a good listener. Encourage others to talk about themselves.
8. Talk in terms of the other person's interests.
9. Make the other person feel important – and do it sincerely.

Each of these principles is easy to do, and the benefits of using them seem powerful in life, not just business.

I wish I could remember these principles by heart, but I don't. That's why I carry this little book with me at all times. They make great sense to me and, again, are rather easy to do. I've read this list of principles dozens of times, and each time I look at these words they confirm that my newly developing style of networking has significant value.

It became clear that Dale Carnegie's principles were going to be a big part of my new idea.

People Who Give

I have heard many quotations related to giving from lots of people who are trusted and respected, not just by me, but by many in the world, today and in the past.

Quotes like:
- "We make a living by what we get. We make a life by what we give." — Winston Churchill
- "No one is useless in this world who lightens the burdens of another." — Charles Dickens
- "It's not how much we give but how much love we put into giving." — Mother Teresa
- "Happiness doesn't result from what we get, but from what we give." — Ben Carson
- "You can give without loving, but you can never love without giving." — Robert Louis Stevenson
- "For it is in giving that we receive." — St. Francis of Assisi
- "Don't wait for other people to be loving, giving, compassionate, grateful, forgiving, generous, or friendly... lead the way!" — Steve Maraboli
- "When it comes to giving, some people stop at nothing." — Vernon McLellan
- "Behold I do not give lectures or a little charity, when I give I give myself." — Walt Whitman
- "It's easier to take than to give. It's nobler to give than to take. The thrill of taking lasts a day. The thrill of giving lasts a lifetime." — Joan Marques
- "Only when you give from the heart does it make the giving whole." — Stephen Richards

These quotations and many more like it speak volumes to me.

I have always known that the Bible verse Luke 6:38, "Give and it shall be given unto you" was real. I learned this as a child watching what my father did. He gave more than he had, and his rewards through life were numerous and real.

As I studied for my new plan, I found lots of other people in my community who believed this. My friends in Toastmasters were not unique. There were many other good people in our community who understood that giving was part of life. Not everyone understood giving first, but those who do reap the benefits of their actions.

My wife and I know this first hand as well. As young parents with little money for unnecessary things, we always managed to give a little to our communities, churches and charities. A few times in our child-rearing period we needed help with doctor bills, car repairs and in at least one instance, the mortgage. We never had to ask for help; it just seemed to happen. The doctors got paid and cars fixed, and the mortgage seemed to always get paid, maybe a little late, but always paid. The money worked out, and it wasn't because someone walked up and handed us money.

It's important for me to admit that there were times when we lost focus on the importance of giving. When this happened, my wife and I could tell that things were harder to do. It seemed harder to make ends meet, and sometimes we faced more challenges. I remember times when we would talk about our challenges and both of us would proclaim "We need to do more for others." We did not have to encourage each other to do this; we always seemed to be in sync on this need.

When we refocused ourselves on giving, without fail,

life seemed to be better.

During my research and planning for a new way to do business, I knew that giving would have to be a big part of what I put together.

Never Eat alone

In 2005, a friend suggested that I read a book called "Never Eat Alone" by Keith Ferrazi.

Don't keep score, build it before you need it, share your passions, follow up or fail, expanding your circle, connect with connectors, stay in touch, be interesting ... these are some of the ideas that Keith shared in his book.

Keith recommends lots of great ideas, philosophies and activities that influenced my ideas and plans to change what I was doing.

Two really important ideas that I learned from Keith's book are:

1 - Never eat alone. Besides being the title of the book, it's also an activity that Keith suggested that we do regularly.

I had always felt that breakfast, lunch and dinners (or after 5 get-togethers of any type) were a good time to meet people and to get to know them. It can be difficult to get to know someone in his office, since most people believe that an office meeting is for talking business. Meeting while having coffee or tea, having a burger and fries or a dinner or drink is a much better environment to talk community, family, friends, life, passion and business.

#2 - Build Relationships. Keith goes into great detail about building relationships in his book.

I knew that this book was going to be a good read after I read the flap introduction. It was exciting and seemed so relevant to my ideas of a different style of networking.

Keith's book was an easy and fun read. He did a good job of telling the reader how to do the things he suggests. He gave great examples of how it has worked for him and others.

Reading "Never Eat Alone" confirmed that I was on the right track with my new ideas of changing my style of networking.

Never eat alone and constantly build relationships - sounded like solid ideas to me, especially after reading Keith Ferrazi's book.

You are not getting the job with that attitude

Enthusiasm and a positive attitude are important when networking.

How many times have you met someone in public who is the opposite of enthusiastic? You know the guy (or gal), who feels that nothing good is going on in his/her life, that everything around him/her and regarding him/her is miserable. You've met these people. They believe that there is no hope for a good life. I've met them hundreds of times, and I refuse to be like them.

We all have stuff going on in our lives. I just refuse to let people outside of my inner circle know about the problems I have to deal with, and I will never share my problems with someone while I am helping them.

I'll never forget the young man who didn't understand this. Because of his attitude, he lost an opportunity to get a job.

I was working for an IT consulting firm in Winston-Salem and had a staffing opportunity that was going to make me good money. But I needed to find the right person for the job.

I phoned screened dozens of good candidates before I found the right guy. He had the experience, education, skills and great references, and he wanted the right amount of money. I arranged to interview him in person.

Our receptionist called my office to let me know that he was in the lobby. She told me that he had showed up on time and was well dressed. I was glad to hear this.

I collected my interviewing materials and headed off to the lobby. Our receptionist heard my first face-to-face meeting with this candidate. This is how it went:

"Hello, I'm Teddy Burriss. How are you doing this morning?"

"Not bad. I wish I could have gotten more sleep, but I'll be OK," replied my candidate.

I responded with a polite "I'm sorry to hear this."

The candidate continued with his whining, "Thanks. Our baby boy was awake all night; I think he is teething. The storms kept our dog pacing the floor all night, and to make the night even worse, my wife was mad at me because I did not take the trash last night. Kind of sucked, but I'll be OK."

I had heard enough. "I was going to interview you this morning for a great job. I think you would be a good candidate for this position. However, I feel that you're not going to be a good candidate today. Please go back home now. Call me tomorrow, and we will reschedule this interview. And there is nothing you can say to change my mind."

I turned and started walking away as he started pleading me to change my mind. I turned around one time and said, "There is no way we are talking any further today. Call me tomorrow. Goodbye."

I could hear him pleading to our receptionist to ask

me to come back. She knew my rule and told him he failed his first impression to me. I could hear her telling him that his best bet was to do as I said and to leave now. He pleaded one more time before she politely said, "Call Mr. Burriss tomorrow, sir."

Even though I hate being around people who are miserable and mad at life, I did not send him home because I didn't want to hear his whining. I sent him home to teach him that he needs to never meet someone for the first time, especially in a job interview situation, without a positive and enthusiastic attitude.

I used to get dragged down by others who hate life. It wore me out trying to keep their miserable attitude from making me miserable, too. I strive to walk away from this misery every chance I get.

Don't misunderstand my point of view. If a friend or even a stranger needs help to overcome an issue, regardless of how small or immense, I will do my best to help him. I believe that I have a good heart and a compassionate ear. When needed I will provide a needed shoulder. But it must be an appropriate time, place and reason.

Meeting someone with the intent of doing business, interviewing for a job or just building a new relationship is not the appropriate time to whine.

The experience with the job candidate reminded me that enthusiasm and a positive attitude are important in the plan I was putting together.

Be careful what you say in public

I love a good joke as much as the next guy. However, you better know what jokes are appropriate when you're networking and building new relationships.

I've had people who I used to consider professional meet me for the first time and commence to tell me off-color, racist, sexist, political and religious jokes.

I've also met people and after a few short conversations they think it's OK to talk bad about other people I may or may not know.

A young woman told me a story about a window salesman who invited into her home and told her, "Our company is serious about your safety. We do background checks and drug tests. There is no way we would ever let a Mexican work on your home." Not only was this an inappropriate statement, hopefully not condoned by the business he worked for, but this guy failed to notice this young mother of three was married to a Mexican. Not only did he ruin his reputation, but he also put a big ugly mark across the brand of the business he worked for.

The young lady kicked him out of her home, proclaiming never to do business with his company and to share his ignorance with others she knew and met. She published his story on her public blog, posted it on Facebook and Twitter.

Why do people think it's OK to speak before thinking?

Regardless of why they feel the need to be rude, disgusting or downright nasty after they think they know me, this is wrong and a major mistake when networking.

When this happens, my opinion of these people takes an immediate and usually irrecoverable downward spiral. I have to wonder who else feels these people are unprofessional. I also struggle with being associated with these people.

I value my reputation too much to jeopardize it by engaging in any kind of inappropriate jokes or gossip. I don't want to be judgmental, but I also want to be cautious and maintain my reputation. Therefore, I strive to distance myself from this behavior.

As I experienced this behavior, I realized that my plan for success should address what I say and do in public as well as who I should or should not associate with.

Networking is not selling

"People buy from people they know and trust." — unknown

"People don't care how much you know, until they know how much you care." — John Maxwell

"A connection does not make a relationship. Giving creates relationships." @NCWiseman

Each of these quotes some value, but when you pull them together the combined meaning is more important.

As I put together my new style of networking, I kept these three quotes in front of me.

I believe in these three quotes and their overall meaning. However, there are some who don't.

Back in 2007, a financial planner sent me this email message:

"Hello, Teddy. Your name comes up often when I am networking. Many of our mutual friends tell me that I should get to know you. Do you have some time in the next few weeks to meet?"

I get messages like this often. I usually agree to a meeting. I agreed to meet with him.

We met at one of my favorite delis in Winston-Salem.

Our conversations started off appropriately. Who are you and who am I discussions. Mostly focused on business, even though I tried to get him to talk more about himself and his career. He did a good job of deflecting the personal questions and turning them into more business chatter.

Within a few minutes he turned the conversation into selling. He pulled out a prospectus on a mutual fund he was hawking. He pulled out a legal pad and began drawing graphs and calculations about my potential revenue if I invested in his programs. He even rattled off names of people he had sold his mutual-fund program to and their "testimonials" of the value.

Then he said the phrase that told me he wanted to sell me rather than get to know me, "I knew when Bill (name changed to protect identity) told me that you were retired that you should see this program."
He must have been talking with a Bill that did not know me; I had not retired.

I had heard enough about his mutual-fund program!

I tried to change the conversation back to our community. He ignored me and went back to talking about his mutual-fund program. He rambled on and on. Not once during his rambling did he ask me a question.

Not only was this guy not a good salesman, he was absolutely a poor networker.

I tried being a little more blunt. "Tom, I appreciate that you believe you have a great mutual-fund program, however I'm not interested in any of these products at this time."

Tom heard what he wanted to hear. "I understand, Teddy. Maybe you would be interested in our annuities." And then he commenced to barf all over me with his annuity-fund program stats.

He failed miserably at networking. It was time for me to end this meeting.

I tried to be polite when I told him that I expected our meeting to be about getting to know each other and not a sales pitch. "Tom, unless you are willing to put away the prospectus information and stop trying to sell me on your funds, I have to go."

Tom was offended. "This is what I do," he said. "I sell financial products to people. I don't have time to waste on chit chat."

Despite my overwhelming desire to get noisy, I tried to stay polite. "I want to say it has been nice to meet you, Tom. I have to go. Have a great day." I walked to the counter, paid for my lunch and left.

I never heard from Tom ever again.

A few years later, I needed to find a financial program to move a 401K into. I liked the company that Tom worked for and considered them. Too bad Tom and I never created any kind of a relationship.

This experience confirmed for me that networking was all about building relationships, not selling.

A new way to network

Networking for Mutual Benefit comes together

It took nearly a year, but I finally had a plan and it made sense.

I had been writing these phrases down for a few years:

"Networking is finding people to help"
"Networking is developing relationships"
"Networking is helping people"
"Networking is all about mutual benefit"
Finally one day I wrote it this way - "Networking is finding, developing and nurturing relationships that mutually move people forward thru life." @NCWiseman

It all finally makes sense to me now.

It's all about meeting people and finding new people to get to know.

It's all about developing a relationship with the folks you meet in life.

It's all about staying in touch or nurturing the relationship.

It's all about giving with no expectation of anything in return.

It's all about connecting with other people when it's appropriate and relevant.

It's all about mutual benefit, not just about me.

It's not about selling or asking for anything until you have permission to ask.

I'd figured it out. Let me share how to do it now.

Growing your circle of connections

In order for Networking for Mutual Benefit to work, you must keep your circle of connections growing.

And, it's much easier and more rewarding when you grow your circle of connections with the phrase "mutually beneficial" in mind.

"The greatest rewards occur when you focus on helping others before you consider your own needs." ~ @NCWiseman

I am a big fan of social media. I connect with people on LinkedIn, Facebook, Twitter and Google+. However, I'm not referring to collecting business cards, LinkedIn connections, Facebook friends, Twitter followers and full Google+ circles   when I say growing your connections. I am referring to connecting with people in a real and meaningful way so as to build a relationship with them.

Yes, connect with as many relevant people as you can through social media. However, you must connect IRL (in real life) as well.

The IRL connections are the most important. These are the people you have conversations with, share ideas, discuss relevant topics and that you help in some way.

Even though IRL requires some kind of ongoing conversations, they do not have to happen face to face. Relationships can develop via phone conversations, email discussions, social media posts and comments, tweets back and forth, etc. I am a little old school and prefer to build relationships face to face, but I have many great virtual relationships as well. Best of all, many of my virtual connections have turned into powerful IRL relationships.

How do you connect with new people? It's not hard and can start with a simple hello in any of these environments:

- Get involved in community activities.
- Get involved in charities, especially on action committees where you can talk with people.
- Go to all of the Chamber of Commerce networking events (business before hours, business after hours, etc.).
- Walk up to a stranger on the street or in the subway and say hello.
- Turn around in the grocery check out and say hello to a stranger.
- Strike up a conversation with someone about an interesting topic.

You must get out of the office. It is way harder to make new connections sitting at your desk and behind a computer screen.

You also have to stop hanging around your close friends and business associates when you are networking. It's OK to hang out with them sometimes, but when your task is to network, ditch your friends for awhile, unless they can introduce you to new people.

Find someone you don't know or don't know much about. Walk up and ask something like:

Hello, what is your name?
What brought you to this event?

Have you been to any other events lately?

Any question relevant to the event or location

NEVER ASK, "What do you do for a living?" This comes later.

Your purpose of striking up a conversation with this new connection is to learn as much about the person as you can. Try to keep the conversation away from business as long as you can. When your new connection sees the conversation turning into business, they will start to fear the stereotypical network barfing, and you never want them feeling this way.

Keep the conversation about the other person as much as you can. Remember the Dale Carnegie principles, and listen to the other person and talk in terms of their interests, not just yours.

If your new connection asks what you do, try to focus on who you are, not what your company is and what it does.

Example: "I'm a electrical engineer. I love to work on challenging engineering projects. What kind of work do you do?"

Answer and return the conversation to your new connection.

Regardless of who you are talking with, the conversation will go into one of three paths:

- There is some apparent relevance between the two of you and another conversation is possible. Strive to find another time to talk more in the near future.
- There is minimal apparent relevance between the two of you, but you may know someone that they should meet. Ask if you can make a relevant introduction for them.

- There is no apparent relevance between the two of you. Be polite and keep the door open for the future when your paths may cross again and you could help each other in some way.

I use the phrase "apparent relevance" because one short conversation may not uncover the real relevance. So never assume that a new connection is completely irrelevant after one conversation. You may uncover some unique and useful relevance in a later conversation.

Always ask your new connection if there is any way you can help him. Focus the offer on the recent conversation. If the conversation allows for it, your new connection may offer the same thing to you. If it is relevant and appropriate to ask, only ask this one question, "Who else do you know that I should meet?" This is not usually appropriate after one conversation; however, a relationship can develop fairly quickly when two good people are talking.

Regardless of how the conversation turns out, I strongly suggest that if you did appropriately share contact information, follow up afterwards and repeat the offer for help with something like this, "I enjoyed our conversation last night. If there is anything I can do to help you in any way, please reach out and contact me."

The other way to keep your circle of connections growing is to ask people you know, trust and respect to introduce you to others they know.

You don't need to get uncomfortable

"The people in you life who you know, trust & respect are the best conduits to other people who you can know, trust & respect." ~ @NCWiseman

Often I hear people say stuff like:

- "I don't like to network."
- "I'm afraid to network."
- "I don't know anyone."
- "I have nothing in common with anyone else."

Bull!!

If you are Networking for Mutual Benefit the right way, it's just a conversation, and most of us can do this without any pain.

Networking for Mutual Benefit does not need to be scary. I can show you how to make it safe.

Networking for Mutual Benefit assumes you know someone, at least a few people. If this is not the case, call me.

We have something in common with more people than we can imagine, until you start Networking for Mutual Benefit and discover the similarities.

One of the easiest ways to get started networking is with the people in our Front Row or our Inner Circle. This group of people can include family and friends. Hopefully, these are the people in our lives whom we trust, respect and care for, people who also trust, respect and care for us. Often there is a mutual love between us and our Front Row. It should be a mutually beneficial relationship.

These people want to know what's going on in our lives, and they want to help us when they can. Make sure they know what you are doing and what kind of people you want to connect with. Far too often we assume that our family and friends are not connected to the people we need to connect with. Maybe they aren't, but they may have good people in their lives who are.

And to make Networking for Mutual Benefit safe, if a good friend knows someone you should know, what are the odds that this new connection will be a fool? Not likely; one of your good friends wants to introduce you to them. Your good friends are not likely to introduce you to a fool or idiot. They like you too much to do this to you.

And to dispel the "We have nothing in common statement," listen to this - Your good friend or family member is friends with this new connection. This is the best commonality ever; you are both friends with another good person. This makes for good conversations. And possibly you will find out that this new connection knows someone else you know. It happens every day for me; I know it will happen for you as well.

To make Networking for Mutual Benefit even better, as you build your relationship with this new connection and because you have a mutual friend, they will not hesitate to ask "What can I do to help you?" All you need to do is ask, "Who else do you know that you think I should know?" It works as long as you are TRUHE (Transparent, Relevant, Useful, Honest and Engaging).

If you want to keep your Networking for Mutual Benefit working for you, never forget that you must give in order to build the relationships. So, never leave a conversation without asking in return, "How can I help you?" If you can, be direct and maybe ask if you can help them with a specific task or activity that they mentioned during the conversations. This is a great way to propel your relationship via Networking for Mutual Benefit.

So, really, you do not need to be uncomfortable when you Networking for Mutual Benefit.

This is the best place to start as you work to grow your circle of connections.

Why? Because these folks are the ones who will most likely understand how you tick and what you are all about. They are the ones who will gladly introduce you to others who could help you. These introductions make powerful connections because you have a mutual connection.

Meet people who are different

In 1978 I worked in Dickerson, Maryland, building a chemical plant. For the most part, the people I hung out with back then were construction workers. We were all very similar in our education and life and work experiences. Our conversations were simple, filled with jokes and teasing each other. It was typical for a bunch of construction workers back then.

In 1988 I worked for a computer company. I begin to spend some time with people in different areas of business: business owners, accountants, HR professionals and operational management employees. I realized these folks had some interesting ideas and very different perspectives about many topics. I learned a lot in this job, mostly through the people that I worked with.

In 1996 I did a lot of traveling as I worked for a company with offices all over the country. The people I met in airports, restaurants, hotels and business offices across the United States were diverse in career and life experiences. These people had even more interesting ideas and perspectives of just about any topic. We talked about subjects I had never discussed in depth with strangers. Topics including politics, religion, economics, marriage, education, business, regional development, etc. Another interesting thing began to happen as I created connections with more unique people; they began to introduce me to other unique and different people. This made the connections, conversations and perspectives even more diverse and interesting.

When I started selling IT solutions in 2005, I again noticed that diversity was important. While I fumbled at networking back then, I began to connect with marketing professionals, private colleges, web designers, software architects, graphic artists, musicians, non-profit directors, business owners, entrepreneurs, etc. The new connections I began to make through this diverse set of connections kept growing with even more diverse connections.

No matter how diverse these new connections were, they all seemed to have one thing in common: Once they trusted and respected me, regardless of our differences, they would do anything they could to help me. And another interesting thing became apparent: The introductions they would make for me were just as diverse and unique as they were themselves. Musicians introduced me to doctors; web developers introduced me to retail shop owners, and software architects introduced me to local government agencies who could use my help or could help me.

It didn't take long to realize that my personal and professional development were directly influenced by the unique and interesting people I met. Diversity of connections was adding lots of value to my networking.

The new and different ideas and perspectives I was learning were important to my growth and success.

This experience taught me that variety is not just the spice of life; it's the opportunity to learn something new, discover new ideas, new perspectives and new opportunities, and meet new friends.

Your Weak Ties

In his book "Never Eat Alone," Keith Ferrazi reminded me of an important group of people who should be included in your networking, both in real life (IRL) and virtually (social media).

These are the people who you have not talked with in six months or longer. These are the people in your community, business and life who respect you, trust you, care for you and maybe even love you. Or at least they used to.

Keith calls these people "Weak Ties."

Yes, I know what some of you are thinking. There are weak ties that need to stay in your past (like the ex-husband, ex-wife, ex-girlfriend or obnoxious former brother-in-law). Don't worry; it's called life.

However, for many different reasons, your weak ties are no longer actively involved in your life or aware of what you are doing. (Hopefully your weak ties are just a result of people getting busy in their lives and not a result of a wrong you did. If this is the case, consider working on fixing the relationship. It could be worth the effort. You'll never know unless you try.)

Your weak ties don't know what's going on in your life. You have no idea what's happening in their lives. Often change has happened in your lives that are both interesting and maybe relevant in some way.

When you reconnect with these folks, you may be

able to help them in some way. They may need your help either directly or indirectly; you don't know unless you reach out to them.

Furthermore, when you do reconnect with these folks, you may find that they are able to help you as well. Don't assume they can't help you based on what you know of their past lives. Their careers and connections may have changed significantly, and therefore, they may be able to help you in some way today.

So how do you reconnect with your weak ties?

You do it the same way you connect with anyone else. Call them, talk with them, invite them to coffee, sweet tea or "soda-30" and ask questions. If you can't get together in person, call and just listen. You have to rebuild your relationship with them because it has diminished. Once you have rebuilt the relationship, you will find that you don't have to ask for anything. Since they used to respect you, trust you, care for you and maybe even love you, they may likely feel this way about you. If so, they'll want to help you any way they can.

I know that my weak ties are important to me. Therefore, each year I send an email to everyone I have an email address for. In this message I say hello, wish them a happy holiday season and remind them to "let me know if I can help you or anyone else in any way." Every year this message results in a renewed relationship and often a few new connections to people that my contacts think would be good for him or me.

Pay attention to your weak ties - they could be powerful in your networking activity and in your life in general.

Building relationships takes time

Some of the sales training programs I attended taught to spend some time on "bonding and rapport" or to make a connection with our prospects by "finding something of relevance" to talk about. Often this area of sales training was a short discussion.

If sales training programs spent more time teaching us bonding and rapport or, more appropriately, "relationship building," I would have better had success doing my sales job.

Create a real relationship with someone, and they are much more likely to take your calls and respond to the email messages. Create a real relationship with someone, and the "gatekeeper" will gladly put your call through. Build an honest relationship with someone, and they will be willing to share ideas and listen to the ideas you want to share with them.

However, creating a real relationship with someone does not happen quickly or easily. It takes time and energy.

As I mentioned in an earlier chapter, the Dale Carnegie principles are important in building relationships. Arousing an eager want for anyone to open up to you only happens when you spend enough time with him. Listening to one conversation with your prospect does not create a relationship.

There is no specific timeframe to building relationships. There are numerous things that can affect the amount of time needed to build an honest relationship.

You must:
- Be transparent at all times;
- Be honest and trustworthy;
- Be engaging and eager to learn what is important to the other person;
- Be perceived as transparent, honest and engaging;
- Be interesting;
- Be able to share relevant and useful information;
- Be able to listen well enough to truly hear what the other person is saying;
- Be able to care enough to give with no expectations or requirements.

All of this takes time and can't happen in a few conversations. Doing these things consistently and frequently increases the power of the relationship. If you are not consistent, then you won't be taken serious in your developing relationship.

However, if you are willing to put the time into building an honest and mutually beneficial relationship, the rewards are many and continual.

In 2005 I met a quiet man during one of my networking events. It was clear that he didn't enjoy networking. We talked for a few minutes while we both worked on shrimp cocktail that was being served. A few months later we met again at another networking event. We talked a little about business, but mostly we talked about our mutual love for good seafood. Before leaving we exchanged business cards, only because he asked for mine. Nearly a year went by before we met again. This time we talked about family, the upcoming elections and a little business. Yes, we again joked about our mutual love for seafood.

Another six months or so went by before we met again. This time my quiet networker asked me about my business. I answered his questions and asked him to tell me more about his business. We discovered that he had a business need that I could likely provide. I asked if we could meet and talk about his needs in detail to determine if I actually had a solution. He agreed. We met later that week and agreed to do business. It took well over a year to get to sales conversations. When we did, it was easier, and there was no long sales dance. This is why I like Networking for Mutual Benefit.

Note: I knew that the company this quiet networker worked for would one day need my help. On the first few times we talked he was not ready to talk business because he was afraid of networking. He told me that lots of sales people pressed him to do business with them, but he decided to do business with me because I first got to know him and allowed him to trust me. Our relationship is thriving; so is the business we do together.

It's all about developing a relationship with the folks you meet in life, regardless of how much time it takes. Eventually the relationship will grow to where it needs to grow.

Not everyone wants a relationship

Does this surprise you? I hope not. It's called life.

Even when Networking for Mutual Benefit, you will meet and talk with people who don't get it and won't change their ways. They only want for themselves and have no desire to help others.

Don't think ill of these folks. That won't benefit you, either.

Remember this:
"God grant me the serenity to accept the things I cannot change; courage to change the things I can; and wisdom to know the difference."

"Don't try to change people for your own benefit. Help them change for themselves." ~ @NCWiseman

If, however, you see some benefit to help them, be honest and focus on helping them.

Introduce them to books from Dale Carnegie, Zig Ziggler, Ralph Waldo Emerson and other great authors with powerful messages.

Then watch what happens. Maybe, just maybe, one day they will catch on and you will be able to build a powerful relationship with them. Never say never; it has happened and can happen again.

Hugging people

One of my good business friends is a lady named Sandy, who is a hugger. When you get to know Sandy, and she knows you, there are no more handshakes. Whenever sees someone she knows, trusts, respects, cares for and likes, she hugs them. There are other men and women who instead of shaking hands with me, would hug me. For most people I do business with, I generally never initiated this physical hello, but I never turned down a hug from a friend. For me, hugging is a much higher level of hello than even a firm handshake. Getting a hug meant that I was trusted, respected and, in many respects, cared for, liked and/or loved by those who hugged me, in life and in business.

When I worked in the IT business, I would announce that I was leaving the office to network by saying "OK, I'm going out to hug people now." My boss was not excited about this. When I first started saying this he would say, "You need to be careful. Most people don't like to be hugged." I'd tell him, "Don't worry. I know what I'm doing."

However, I meant, for the most part, metaphorically hugging, not physically hugging. If I worked hard at building honest and real relationships with people, they would trust, respect, care for and like me enough to want to physically or metaphorically hug me. I wanted to create relationships with the people I was doing business with so that they wanted to either physically hug me, or at least, metaphorically hug me.

Many a candidate has hugged me for helping them to

get a job. Many a hiring manager or HR person has hugged me for helping them to find the right candidate.

A few years ago a business contact asked me to help a friend of hers borrow printers, copiers and computers for a charitable event. It was not something that I was able to directly help her with. I spent just under an hour asking my connections for help, and I was able to find companies in the area that had the ability to provide the equipment that this charity needed. Both my business friend and the lady who ran the charitable event thanked me with big hugs. I had never met the charity lady before. Today, we are all good friends and help each other often, and I do business with the charity.

Granted, most of the hugs I get in business are metaphorical, but they are just as important as the physical hugs.

Go out and hug someone today. There are plenty of hugs to go around once you are trusted respected and liked. And a hug can create powerful mutually beneficial relationships.

A hug does not have to be physical, but it does have to be given freely with no expectations of something in return.

A new way to cold call

I'm am not afraid of cold-calling people who don't know me, but I enjoy calling people who know, trust and respect me. They'll talk to me.

Cold-calling people you don't know is something that all sales people had to do.

However, when I started Networking for Mutual Benefit, I started making lots of new connections, and many of them were people who I knew could use my services.

While first meeting these people, I tried to stay out of the sales mode. I worked hard at getting to know them, listened to their stories about themselves and their jobs or businesses. We often exchanged business cards, but I resisted cold-calling them until after I had begun building a relationship with them.

Remember, a connection does not make a relationship, and you need a relationship before you can ever ask for anything.

Often the relationships began in the next conversation, over coffee or during a social event. Sometimes they began through a follow-up email where I always ask, "Let me know if there is anything I can do to help you."

Often the relationship started developing after I did something simple to help the other person. Just as frequently all I had to do was to introduce them to someone who was able to solve a problem that I couldn't solve.

The third most often relationship building activity was for me to help someone else's friend or family member. As Dale Carnegie said, "One of the best ways to make a friend is to do something nice for their family member."

Each time I did something nice or "gave" in any way, I would get a new connection who could do something for me. As a salesperson, this was usually an introduction to a business that could use my services.

Here are a few examples.

- A friend introduced me to the controller of a local company. He found out that I volunteer at job search network groups and asked me to help a friend. Within a few weeks, he said, "How can I help you, Teddy." Eventually he introduced me to the VP of sales and marketing, who I had to call to arrange a meeting.
- A member of a charitable board I am on appreciated the work I did to help the charity create new sponsorship programs. He told me, "I want to help you in return for your good work Teddy. How can I help you?" Soon thereafter, I got a meeting with the VP business development for his community bank, after I called him for a meeting.
- A neighbor introduced me to her good friend who is the IT Manager at a small business in town. Because I had helped his friend with some basic PC problems (probably helped him indirectly as well), he invited me in to learn about his business. He introduced me to the director of IT, who I had to call for a meeting.
- And, don't forget the lady I worked with on the March of Dimes committee. She liked me so much

that she put my business card on her husband's side of the bed, with a note saying, "I Love this Guy!" That call was far easier; he called me. (I'll tell you more about this story later.)

In each of these cases, I still had to call the person to arrange for a meeting. Each call became a conversation. And each conversation resulted in a well-received invitation to meet and discuss business.

I so much more enjoy calling people who know who I am and are willing to talk. It beats cold calling every day.

Give with no expectations is powerful

I don't like the phrase "Scratch my back and I'll scratch yours." Why? Because the words clearly show that there is an expectation, and I will never give with an expectation of something in return. And I don't like it when others do this, either.

On the other hand, I am a fan of the The Golden Rule, "Do unto others as you would have them do unto you." This proverb is derived from the Bible verse - Matthew 7:12 - "Therefore all things whatsoever ye would that men should do to you, do ye even so to them."

I personally believe that "Giving is a powerful way to build relationships. However, if you give with even the slightest expectation of something in return, this is bartering, not giving." @NCWiseman

Every day I strive to give, to help, to be a servant and to do for others when they can't do for themselves. I know that giving creates real value for me over time. I have no problem saying that "Giving makes money for me."

When I am talking with anyone, a new or old friend or business associate, I focus on how I can help him first. Often I do something to help someone else as a result of our conversations and in case you missed this statement; I never expect anything in return.

At the voting polls in 2012, I ran into a distant friend I hadn't seen in nearly a year. We agreed to have coffee the following week. During our conversation she shared with me lots of stuff that was important to her. Her job had become stressful; her family was facing challenging times, and she was not sure what to do. We talked at length, and I shared with her ideas when she asked me to.

When we ended our conversation, I asked her to stay in touch with me and to reach out to me if there was anything I could do to either help her or introduce her to someone who could. She was very grateful for my time and an offer to help. Even though she works for an organization that I would love to do work with, I did not ask her for anything and I had no expectations that she will ever say "Teddy, what can I do to help you?"

It's not important to me. It's important that she knows that I cared enough to focus on her needs and not try to sell her or ask for something for myself.

The help that I give others is usually not difficult, expensive or strenuous. It can be as simple as listening or introducing them to someone else. It could be physical, such as putting in a fence or moving furniture, but not usually. It could be buying lunch, a soda or cup of coffee, just because I want to. Sometimes it's as simple as sharing an interesting idea or connecting them to someone else who has what they need or want. Regardless of what I do, it's a form of giving with no expectation of anything in return.

When I am networking in a meeting or in a one-on-one conversation, I strive to find a way to give as well.

I know many business folks don't agree with me. Many will say, "You are supposed to be networking to uncover an opportunity to sell, not to be giving stuff away." Yeah, I disagree and not respectfully.

I believe in the Bible verse, Luke 6:38 - "Give, and it shall be given unto you; good measure, pressed down, and shaken together, and running over, shall men give into your lap. For with the same measure that you measure it shall be measured to you again."

I learned a long time ago that the rewards I get for doing good will come when I least expect it and from someone that I would not expect the reward from. Some call it karma; some call it God's blessings on me. I call it a fact of life.

I don't want to box you in with ideas of giving because giving should be broad, diverse and relevant to you and your relationships. One person's ability to give is different than another's. We are all unique and different individuals with unique and different abilities and desires to give.

Giving has to be all about the other person and not about us. If we give only because we believe it may help us, this is selfish and will "jinx," distort or ruin the real benefit and rewards of giving.

If you think someone will wonder "Did he help me because he wants something in return," then you are likely not giving the right way.

Some of the best rewards I have received from others start with, "Hey, Teddy. Your name came up in a conversation today."

It's that simple. When you help others and they know you are doing it because you care, your name will come up often. The rewards start to happen when your name comes up in conversations with people you have never met before.

I am regularly introduced to people who need my services, and the introductions come from people I may have helped years ago.

Call it Karma, God's blessings or just a fact of life; it works.

It's all about giving with no expectation of anything in return.

My Contacts are like Gold

My Rolodex is one of my most treasured personal belongings.

OK, I hope it's not hard to believe that I don't own a Rolodex. I also don't collect business cards in those old plastic business-card holders.

However, I have a great collection of contact information that I honor and respect in every way possible. I collect this information in my Contacts folder within my Google account. This gets me instant access to them anywhere I am from my SmartPhone, Mac or from any computer in the world.

When I meet someone new and decide that there is a reason to contact him at a later time, I politely ask for his business card. I never give out my business card unless there is a clear reason for us to connect at a later time. This is the ritual I perform when I get a business card from someone, or meet someone online and get her contact information via email.

I enter all of their contact information into my Contacts system.
I send an email back to the new connection and thank them for connecting with me. I will reference the conversations or interaction that we met through.

I then search LinkedIn for my new contact. If I find them there, I send a LinkedIn connection request using the option "Other" and her email address. I put a relevant and interesting note in the "Personal Note" area of the connect request so that my new connection knows that I am excited about making the connection IRL (In Real Life) as well as virtually through LinkedIn.

If I have a business card, I file it away in a big plastic bucket. I'm working on my second bucket now.

Now that I have all of my contacts at my fingertips at all times, I can contact them when needed and, more importantly, I can connect them to each other when needed and appropriate.

My contacts are treasured belongings to me.

Connecting people is powerful

One of the best ways to "give" is to introduce someone to another person who may benefit from the introduction, or where a mutually beneficial relationship could develop. In many respects I think connecting people is the most powerful giving I can do.

Before I share some examples of connecting people, let me say this:

I am deliberate about connecting people. I strive to always make the introductions transparent, honest, useful, relevant and engaging. I call this TRUHE, Transparent, Relevant, Useful, Honest and Engaging/ Entertaining. If I don't subscribe to my TRUHE philosophy, then my introductions would be less valuable, a lesser relationship and more likely only about selling something. I refuse to treat my contacts this way.

Here is a bad example of connecting people:

At least a few times a year a new connection will contact me with an invitation to coffee or lunch. Since I am always interested in new and possibly mutually beneficial connections, I almost always agree. (I strive to stay focused, so when needed I will push a less relevant meeting out into the future.)

During our chat, someone who doesn't know me well will inevitably ask, "Let's look at your LinkedIn connections or your personal contacts and find four or five people you can introduce me to today." There is not

a chance in the world that I will do this. Here is why:
- I don't know enough about this new contact;
- I don't know enough about his business;
- My contacts that I have already have a relationship with trump my new contacts every day.

Worst of all, it appears that my new contact isn't trying to build a relationship with me; he is just after my contacts.

I try to explain this to those who "ask" for access to my connection list before they create a relationship with me. I encourage my new contact to be patient. Some get it, while some seem appalled that I would impose my relationship requirement on them. I have learned to be thankful when they get it and to not get upset when they don't. Remember the Serenity Prayer?

God grant me the serenity to accept the things I cannot change;
courage to change the things I can;
and wisdom to know the difference.

However, the new people I meet who are active in the community, show up at events I participate in, engage properly through social media and who help others, these are the people I notice the most. These people are top of my mind. When I see a need to connect two people, they are the ones that I think of first. I love to see a new connection get past scouring connection lists and get engaged to build relationships.

Here are some good examples of connecting people:

- Helping unemployed friends meet hiring managers I know well vs. just forwarding their resume;
- Helping a business owner I know well find a resource to complete a pressing and challenging project;

- Introducing a pregnant friend to a family that no longer needs baby furniture and clothes;
- Connecting a college grad with a startup that needs an eager intern;
- Introducing a business owner with investment money to an entrepreneur who has a dream.

Remember, I only connect people when appropriate, relevant and it could be mutually beneficial for both of them.

All of these people connecting activities, and many more have been very rewarding for me. It was primarily because I helped someone who needed the help. However, despite the fact that I never expected anything in return, connecting people has helped me equally as much. It was often not directly because of the introduction, but indirectly and after the fact.

Helping people to get jobs has helped me to meet business owners who need my help;

Helping a business owner find another resource, from another company, has helped me to get into discussions about the services I was able to provide;

Helping a pregnant friend find free furniture has helped me to get a meeting with her husband who needed my services later on;

Connecting a college grad to an internship opened the door for me to do work with his sister at another business;

Introducing venture capital money to an entrepreneur helped him get funding for the work that I did with him.

However, it's important to know that I introduce people not for the reward or glory, but to help. I benefited later only because: Some call it Karma, some call it God's blessings. I call it a fact of life.

If it's first about me it will fail

"What we do for ourselves dies with us. What we do for others and the world, is and remains immortal." ~ Albert Pine

"We all should rise, above the clouds of ignorance, narrowness, and selfishness." ~ Booker T. Washington

I love quotes like this because they remind me to not get so wrapped up in myself, but to instead focus on helping others.

As I have always said, "Doing good and helping others is a great way to become successful."

Conversely, selfishness creates failure. Not just within a single action or task, but in life. I remember times when I knew I was being selfish. Not only did the task or action not work as well as I hoped, but later on Karma, God's will and/or life in general bit me in the butt as well.

In 1997 I bought a house in Advance, North Carolina. The refrigerator was supposed to convey in the purchase, but the day of settlement I walked the property and saw the refrigerator was gone. The owner claimed that it was an old refrigerator and thought that I would not want it, so he threw it away. I was so mad that I demanded $1,000 to replace the refrigerator, even though I knew it was an old appliance likely only worth a few hundred dollars. My wife told me that I was being unrealistic and even unfair with my demands, but I stuck to my demand.

The seller reluctantly agreed to my demands, and after settlement, I went to a local appliance store and bought myself a thousand-dollar refrigerator. Top of the line, biggest fridge in the store. Man, I was gloating in my reward, or at least I thought I was.

The next day the appliance center delivered the refrigerator, and it would not fit into the house. They had to take the doors off in order to get it through the front door.

When they finally got it into the kitchen, it would not fit into the space where the old refrigerator was. The delivery guys were laughing at me. I thought for sure I heard one of them ask me, "Where do you want your big fancy refrigerator, Mr. Burriss?" My wife said no one ever said that, out loud.

The refrigerator sat in the middle of the kitchen for three days until I finished cutting the cabinets and counter top to make room for it. I estimated that the cost of changing the kitchen to accommodate my reward was likely in the area of $400 to $500.

All because I got selfish and greedy because the homeowner had thrown away an old refrigerator worth maybe a few hundred dollars.

Karma, God's will, or maybe it was just life bite me in the butt with that one.

One day in August of 2006 I made my ninth or 10th cold call to the IT director of a large insurance company in Winston-Salem. Monthly, I would call this guy and usually ended up leaving the same voicemail message, "Hello, Mr. IT Guy. I am Teddy Burriss of XYZ IT company in Winston-Salem. We sell brand ABC of

Hardware and Software, and I would love to meet you and show you how we can save your company money while improving your business." I always felt that this was a selfish call to be making, but I had to do what the boss told me to do.

Later that day I got a call back from a lady who worked for this insurance company. She told me that her boss wanted me to meet with her and to explain to her what we do. I was so excited. We arranged to meet the next day. We met in her cubicle where I told her all about our business, products and successes.

I talked for nearly 20 minutes before I asked her to tell me about her job. This is when I realized that I had been set up. She was an AP clerk and had nothing to do with the IT Projects that I wanted to propose. She was pretending to know what I was talking about and even to care about it. It hit me like a ton of bricks. The IT director set me up. He never told me directly, and I never heard it from anyone else, but I was sure that the IT director sent me on a wild-goose chase because I selfishly and repeatedly called him trying to get an appointment, for me, not him.

As I walked out of their building I could hear them all laughing at me. Maybe they weren't, but it felt this way. Again, karma, God's will, or maybe it was just life biting me in the butt again.

Networking for Mutual Benefit has to be all about the other person.

Do you have permission to ask?

Cold calling is the process of contacting prospects, either via phone, email or now through social media, who are not expecting such an interaction.

Most sales people believe the purpose of cold calling is to get an opportunity to introduce your business and products to someone new. "Asking" for this opportunity when you have not been given permission is why it's such a difficult task.

For this reason I recommend that you work on getting permission from your prospects before asking for anything.

Getting permission is also much more enjoyable than cold calling or trying to sell to someone you don't know.

I like to network to meet people, to learn and discover ideas and to build relationships. Not to sell. Let me repeat this because it is so important - I DO NOT NETWORK TO SELL!

Regularly while networking someone will walk up to me and launch into their sales pitch about their products. And with no regard for my needs or interest they continue trying to sell me on their company and products. Has this ever happened to you?

Another thing that happens frequently while networking is someone will ask me to introduce them to someone I know. Usually this request is in an effort to make a sales pitch or to get a job. More often than not, this request comes from people I barely know or have no professional or personal relationship with.

I met a lady who I knew worked for a business that needed my help. We agreed to have breakfast one morning.

When we got together we talked about lots of different topics, mostly about her career and the work that she does.

I listened as she told me about her college career, transition from one business into the banking industry and her career path to senior manager of business development for a large regional bank.

She asked about me, so I told her about my journey through corporate America before I started my own business.

We talked about family and personal goals. The conversation went on for nearly two hours before we both realized how much time had gone by.

I asked her to tell me what I could do to help her and she said I had already done so. Our conversation had gotten her thinking about her career and life. She asked me to stay in touch because she knew that one day we would do work together.

She never asked, "What can I do to help you, Teddy?" This question never came up at all, not even indirectly. Therefore, I decided not to ask her for anything.

After our breakfast meeting I sent her an email thanking her for a great conversation and offering, again, to help her any way I could.

A few months went by before I heard back from her. She sent me an email asking me to meet her and the vice president of sales and marketing for the bank. Eventually, I signed an agreement to do work with the bank.

I asked this lady after our first project, "What made you call me for this work?" She said, "You listened to me and cared about me. You were not selfish or trying to sell me. I like people who care first."

Remember:

A. Networking is not for selling – NEVER.
B. You can not ask for anything unless you have permission – PERIOD.
C. You can't ask for permission, it must be given to you – ALWAYS.
D. You can only be given permission after you have begun building a relationship – BAM.

Today, I have a great relationship with this lady and am doing lots of work with the bank she worked for. Today, she is working for another organization and has already reached out to me for a new project.

This experience is a great example of "build the relationship first; the sales will come soon enough."

Don't ask for something you don't know exists

When you ask for something that can't be given to you, you are likely to hear, "I'm sorry. I can't help you."

These or similar words are tough words that, when uttered, create a barrier between you and the person you just asked.

Often while networking I see this happen regularly. People who don't understand Networking for Mutual Benefit will ask for things like:

- Can I tell you about my products and services? When there is no need for them.
- Can I give you a copy of my resume? When there is no job.
- Can I give you our donation materials and form? When there is no money in the budget.
- Come to my MLM event, everyone needs a second revenue stream. When there is no desire or interest at all.
- Let me tell you about a retirement program I think you may need. When there is no need.
- I think your business can benefit from my company's expertise. When they don't know much about each other.
- Introduce me to five of your connections so I can sell my stuff. When there is no relationship or trust yet.

When networking, you have to first work to build relationships with the people you are connecting with before you can ask for anything. Once you have this relationship, whether simple or refrigerator privilege, there is one question that you will want to ask before any other.

Don't ask, "Who do you know who can buy my stuff?" or "Who do you know that would be interested in my products?"

Instead, ask an easier question: "Who else do you know that would be a good connection for me?"

Phrase the statement clearly so that your connection understands. "I'm not asking you who can buy my stuff, or who has a job. I only want to meet other people whom you feel would be good connections for me as I build my business, or consider new job ideas, people with ideas and even different perspectives."

If needed, add some more clarity by saying, "Even people you think I could help in some way."

Meeting new people is how you grow your network and find new ideas, opportunities and even friends. Once you have permission to ask, always ask for help to meet more people you can develop even the simplest of relationships with.

It's OK to ask, "Can I tell you about my business, products and/or services" once you know that there may be an interest and you have permission to ask.

It's OK to ask, "Can we talk about the job opening you have" once you know that there is a job and you have permission to ask.

Otherwise, once you have permission to ask, unless the door has been opened for those other questions, you should only ask, "Who else do you know that would be a good connection for me?"

It's far more rewarding to ask for something that may exist.

You have to Sell

For most people who network, the primary reason is to sell their stuff. Otherwise, the bills don't get paid and the desired lifestyle can't be realized.

For others, networking may be about finding a job. Without a job or way to create revenue, life is far more difficult in many ways.

Networking can be the preface to new business opportunities, volunteering, community involvement, making new friends or just about anything to do with people.

Regardless of the primary reason for networking, it's important to remember to go to the next step only after beginning to build relationships.

Networking for Mutual Benefit is just the first big step.

Having great selling skills is important, if not critical, to the process of closing business. You need to know how to help your prospect uncover pain, determine her budget and understand the prospect's buying process all the while trying to drive the process yourself.

Knowing who you are and how you can bring value to an organization as an employee, contractor or consultant is paramount when you get to the job discussion, phone screening or interviews.

Being clear about your other activities, goals or

commitments is also important.

However, remember to focus on the honest steps of Networking for Mutual Benefit, before you start the selling, asking for a job, business opportunity, etc.

Networking for Mutual Benefit
success stories

There is no doubt in my mind that Networking for Mutual Benefit works. My life and business are rewarding and successful because I always Network for Mutual Benefit.

Here are a few stories of people successfully using Networking for Mutual Benefit.

Story # 1 - Nigel Alston, a good friend in Winston-Salem, shared this story with me.

Curtis is a friend and former colleague from our days together at GMAC Insurance (formerly Integon Insurance). Several years ago, he told me that he was looking for an opportunity closer to home. His position at the time was with an out-of-state company.

In a conversation with another friend – a business management consultant and retired corporate executive - I learned of a search he was leading for a new CEO of an organization through his company. He asked if I knew of a qualified candidate, and Curtis immediately came to mind.

I facilitated the connection that eventually led to Curtis applying for and later being offered the position. A mutual need was met that positively benefited both parties. Curtis moved closer to home, and a position was filled with a qualified candidate.

Curtis and I regularly stay in contact with each other,

so it was not a surprise to hear about an opportunity to lead a strategic planning retreat for a group he was contracted to provide management services. He recommended me to them for the project. I was approved to do the work, and, after leading a productive session, more work is likely to follow.

Following my note of thanks to Curtis for the opportunity, along with a summary of our work together, he sent me this note: "Thank you, Nigel, for a well planned and executed session."

Our network for mutual benefit continues to thrive in expected and unexpected ways.

This is a great example of what Networking for Mutual Benefit is all about. Friends are helping friends.

Nigel Alston

Story # 2 - Sandy Jolley, another good friend in Winston-Salem shared this story with me:

My job at Goodwill Industries of Northwest North Carolina came from Networking for Mutual Benefit.

While working at Le Bleu in Winston-Salem, I met Tempy of Goodwill. We were members of the Winston-Salem Chamber of Commerce Referral Group called "Triad Synergy." We got to know each other and quickly became friends. I helped introduce Tempy to businesses that she needed to meet. Tempy repeatedly told me that she wanted to help me "any way I can." When I left Le Bleu, Tempy introduced me to her boss, and they hired me on the spot. It was all because Tempy and I became friends through our networking.

Story # 3 - Megan Gioeli of M.Gioeli Photography

shared this story with me a earlier in 2012.

Author disclosure - Megan is one of my daughters. She never listened to me about Networking for Mutual Benefit as a child. She thought her Daddy was crazy.

It started with "Hi."

I was standing in a long line at Jo-Ann fabrics about eight months ago when I met "M". She was standing behind me in line and we started up a causal conversation. I asked her what project she was working on. Come to find out she owns a company where she makes pocketbooks out of recycled materials (old ties, leftover fabrics, etc.). I told her I was a photographer, and we chatted for a while longer, waiting in the long line. We decided that since we would soon be at the check out, we would exchange business cards.

Later that night I noticed she "Liked" my photography page on Facebook. She then sent me a Friend Request, which I accepted. A few weeks later, she called to ask if I would take pictures at her daughter's first birthday party that was coming up in a few months. She agreed to my fee with no hesitation.

At the birthday party she introduced me to many of her friends and family. Once I finished her birthday party images, I posted a few on my photography Facebook page and tagged her. Her friends and family commented on many of them with great comments about the quality of the pictures and how great the party was. Because of these pictures and the social media activity, I got a bunch of new "likes" on my business page that weekend. One of M's friends, L, emailed me about doing a session for her son and daughter soon after the birthday party pictures were posted. I now have booked several different photo sessions with L. She now refers to me as her family photographer. L's friend A contacted me a month later because she loved the pictures she saw of L and M. She asked about my newborn packages. She signed up for this program. I will get to photograph her family for at least the next year. A told her friend AG, who is also pregnant and now she wants to sign up for a maternity package. A few weeks, later M also introduced me to a friend named P, who crochets and knits. P and I are now doing work together. She is making hats, blankets and other baby clothing for me to use in my photography work. I provide her images so she can market her products online.

All of these new contacts and friends came because I turned around to say hi to someone in line at the store. I like Networking for Mutual Benefit.

Story # 4 - Richard Serge shared this story with me in late 2012:

I know that Networking for Mutual Benefit works. Here is one story of many that I could share with you.

My first job as a designer came through a relationship I had developed with an instructor at Winston-Salem State University.

We talked a lot during and after class and quickly determined that we had some of the same interests.

After the semester ended, we kept in touch. Sometime later, he got a job with ModaCAD Inc. in High Point. The company was new to the area and was building staff. They needed to add a photographer/ designer, so my instructor friend from college called me and asked if I would be interested in the job. I was, and a meeting with the director was scheduled soon afterward.

When I got to the office, my friend introduced me to some of his coworkers and the work they were doing. This really made me feel at ease, right before the interview. Everyone was really nice. I did not have any stress going into the interview because of the introductions my friend made for me. During the interview I offered a copy of my resume to the manager. He said, "We don't need that." Without looking at my resume, they gave me an offer within a few minutes.

A few years later, the HR manager called me asking for my resume. They needed to have a copy on file.

I was glad to have made good connections and gotten this job. I got the job solely on the recommendation of a friend that I made while in college.

Story # 5 - Here is a story I want to share with you.

I have never had an interview, background check or drug test.

Every job I have ever gotten came from conversations with people I knew, trusted and respected and because to some level, they knew, trusted and respected me.

My first job out of college came from a friend who told his boss I would be a good hire.
My job at the chemical plant came because a neighbor told me about the job and asked if I wanted to go to work for him.
I got a job at my first IT company because the business manager at the chemical plant and I became

friends and he hired me to help him start his business.

I got my job in the grass-seed industry because of a business relationship with the controller of the company in New Jersey.

My next job came when the owner of the grass-seed company told the new owners in North Carolina that I would be a great asset to them.

My Las Vegas job came because the owners of the grass-seed company recommended me for the position.

When the Las Vegas company folded, the company in North Carolina created a new position for me because they wanted me back in their organization.

Here is the story of how I got my next IT company job:

In the summer of 2005, I told a few close friends that I wanted to change careers. I had to be discrete about this job search because I had to carefully plan my exit from the current job.

I got together with good friends weekly at a Winston-Salem Toastmaster's club. I had developed a good relationship with one of the ladies in this club. I confidentially told her about my plans, and she said, "If I can help you in any way, let me know." I told her, "If you know anyone that I should talk to regarding a new career idea, please let me know." Within a week she came to me with an idea.

Her boss was looking for a new senior business developer, and she knew that he would want to add me to his team. She had already told him about me, and he was so eager that he called me within 15 minutes of me telling my friend I would talk with him.

This lady knew me, trusted me and cared for me. We

were friends helping each other in our Toastmasters club. Her introduction of me to her boss was for the most part all he needed to hire me. We met numerous times and each time all he did was tell me about his business. He asked few questions about me, my talents or my experiences. He never asked for a resume or references. I got the job because he trusted and respected my friend enough to trust her recommendation.

I eventually ended up working for my friend, and I did anything she asked because I appreciated the introduction she made for me to get my job. It was a great job where I learned a lot. Most of all, I developed my Networking for Mutual Benefit and Building Relationships through social media in this sales job.

I never applied online for a job or mailed resumes blindly to any company. Every job came from good connections that resulted from good Networking for Mutual Benefit activity.

And I still have never had an interview, background check or drug test. (They should have done a background check and drug test on me. Just joking.)

Story # 6 - Here is another story I want to share. It's the best Networking for Mutual Benefit story ever. I mentioned it earlier.

Working on a charitable committee:

I spent many years working on a committee for the local March of Dimes. Year after year I sat beside a lady during the North Carolina Chili Championship committee meetings. We'll call her Sue.

This was one of the biggest events in Winston-Salem

and involved hundreds of hard-working people. The last year of this event was bittersweet. Sue and I were talking about all the great stuff we did together and how much we learned about each other.

I tried hard to keep my professional IT sales work separate from the work with the March of Dimes. It was not important or relevant. During our last meeting together, Sue asked, "Teddy, what do you do for a living?"

I told her about my IT sales work. Sue said, "I love working with you, Teddy. Is there anything I can do to help you?" My response was quite simple. "I want to meet as many IT professionals as possible so that they know what I do and can consider me as a resource for them."

What happened next was so far from believable, but I swear it's true.

Sue said, "My husband is the director of IT for ABC Incorporated (I do not have permission to say the company name)." Wow, this company was on my target list, and I had not found a way to get to them yet. I told her that I would love to meet her husband.

Sue asked for my business card, which I gave her. She wrote on the back of my business card, "I love this guy!" My immediate response was, "Please don't get me in trouble with your husband."

Sue said, "He'll be OK with this, and I'm sure he'll call you when he sees where I leave the card."

I again said, "Come on, Sue. I'd really like to talk with your husband, not get punched out by him." She said, "Trust me, Teddy. When he finds your business on his pillow in our bed he'll call you and talk with you. It'll be OK." I was scared, but I trusted her.

Sure enough, the next morning her husband called me and said, "My wife loves you. You must be a good guy. Let's talk."

Story # 7 - I have to share this story of how I got to work with the Forsyth Technical Community College Small Business Center.

For five years while I worked for the IT company, I attended many events at the Winston-Salem Chamber of Commerce. Nearly weekly I would go into the chamber building to attend an event there. As I entered the building I often glanced to the right and would see the two women in the Small Business Center office of Forsyth Tech Community College. Usually I would wave at them, smile and head off to the chamber meetings.

One day in early 2011, after I started my business, I was in downtown Winston-Salem for a meeting. I had to use the restroom before my meeting and was too far away from any public places. However, I was outside of the chamber building and had plenty of time.

I walked into the building, did my normal glance to the right and waved at the lady sitting at the front desk. She waved back.

I walked up to the front door of the Chamber of Commerce offices and discovered they were closed. What to do? I know. I'll go to the Small Business Center offices. They share restrooms.

I walked into their offices and asked, "May I use your restroom key?"

The lady I now know as Thea said, "Sure."

Seeing the keys hanging in the corner, I grabbed the one marked "Men" and went about my business.

I returned and hung the key back in its place. I turned to the Thea and asked, "What do you do here?"

She asked my name and said, "We support small businesses as they get started."

I asked her, "Who runs this center?"

"Nell Perry does," Thea said.

"Is she here, and, if so, can I say hello to her?" I asked.

Thea picked up the phone and called Nell Perry. I heard her quietly say, "Some guy named Teddy Burriss is here to see you."

"Nell said to come back to her office," Thea said as she hung up the phone and pointed down the hallway.

I walked down the hall as Nell came around the corner to greet me.

When we met I said, "Hi, Nell. I'm Teddy Burriss."

Her response blew me away. "I know who you are, Teddy Burriss. You have walked past my office for five years, yet you have never come in here to say hello."

To make a long story shorter, we talked for nearly two hours about what the Small Business Center does, their need for business coaches and instructors and my desire to help wherever I can.

I immediately began volunteering as a business coach and within three months I was on the calendar delivering seminars on Networking for Mutual Benefit, Building Relationships through Social Media, blogging and Prezi.com.

Wow, I wish that I had stopped in and said hello to Nell five years earlier. She is now a good friend and business partner.

No longer do I walk past someone more than a few times without stopping and saying hello. I've learned that you miss out on a lot if you don't stop.

These are only a few of the success stories that show that Networking for Mutual Benefit works. If you focus on helping others first, you will create real relationships that help you later on.

Join me by living the edict, "Networking is finding, developing and nurturing relationships that mutually move people forward through life."

Bringing it all together

In summary:

Networking used to be:

- Collecting business cards;
- Barfing all over each other hoping to spew the right stuff at the right time to the right person who may need my stuff;
- Desperately looking for someone to buy our stuff and barfing all over them, even when they are not interested;
- Meeting as many people in one hour as humanly possible, with no for their feelings;
- Cold-calling anyone regardless of any relevance or need;
- Groping through each other's contact list while doing the one-on-one dance.

I can't imagine ever doing this again. Today it seems like such a waste of time. Networking this way feels selfish.

Networking for Mutual Benefit is:

- Meeting new people every day;
- Striving to build a relationship with them, either simply or completely to refrigerator privileges;
- Helping others and giving with no expectations;
- Constantly working on building your circle of contacts;
- Connecting others who can mutually benefit from a new connection;
- Nurturing and developing your connections through the power of giving;
- Focusing on another's needs instead of our own;
- Never asking for anything until you have permission to ask;
- With permission, only asking, "Who do you know that I need to meet next and who do you know that I can help?"
- Never barfing your business, products, solutions, features and benefits on anyone;
- Creating mutually beneficial relationships so that you can help each other;
- Only selling or asking for anything once you have a relationship and you know there is a need;
- Networking is all about "finding, developing and nurturing relationships that mutually move people forward through life." ~@NCwiseman

Is Networking for Mutual Benefit easy? **It can be**!

Does it happen overnight? **NO!**

Is it a lifestyle? **YES!**

Are there some people you won't be able to develop relationships with? **Yes**!

Invest the time and energy into growing your circle of contacts, nurture them by giving and helping where you can, building relationship first, and the benefits will occur.

Done correctly and the powers of karma, God's blessings and/or life will create opportunities, open doors and help you to succeed where ever you put your focus.

I learned this later in life, mostly because I had jumped into a sales job with no idea how to do it. I wish that I had learned this far earlier in life. Not that I wish my life was different or better, but that maybe I could have helped far more people and created far more relationships.

Networking without mutual benefits works; however Networking for Mutual Benefit is far more rewarding, enjoyable and successful.

Hopefully after reading this book you will share it with others. Maybe, just maybe, I can help more people through this book.

Maybe together we can change the world.

Connect with me

If you have not already figured it out, I love to connect with new people, and I am a big fan of building relationships through social media.

It would not be polite if I didn't tell you how and where to connect with me.

Email - NCWiseman@TeddyBurriss.com

Facebook Profile - www.facebook.com/TLBurriss

NCWiseman on Facebook -
    www.facebook.com/NCWiseman

LinkedIn Profile - www.linkedin.com/in/TLBurriss

Business LinkedIn Page
    www.linkedin.com/burrissconsulting

NCWiseman LinkedIn Group
    www.linkedin.com/groups?gid=4457273

"Are you Listening to Me?" - www.tlburriss.com

"Notes from NCWiseman" - www.ncwiseman.com

If you have any questions or suggestions about Networking for Mutual Benefit and/or this book, please reach out to me and share or ask. I enjoy great conversations and ideas from the people I connect with.

25519304R00069

Made in the USA
Lexington, KY
26 August 2013